AF575891

HIPPOCRATES

MARCIA AMIDON LUSTED

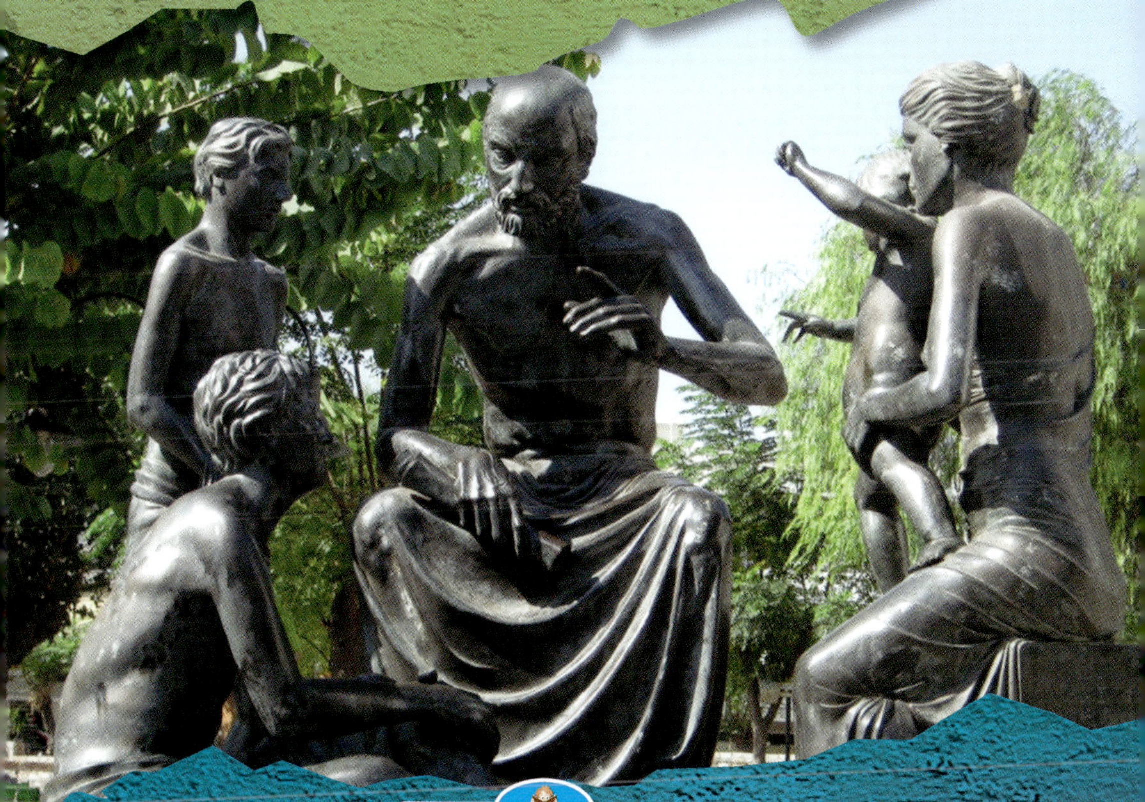

Mitchell Lane
PUBLISHERS
2001 SW 31st Avenue
Hallandale, FL 33009
www.mitchelllane.com

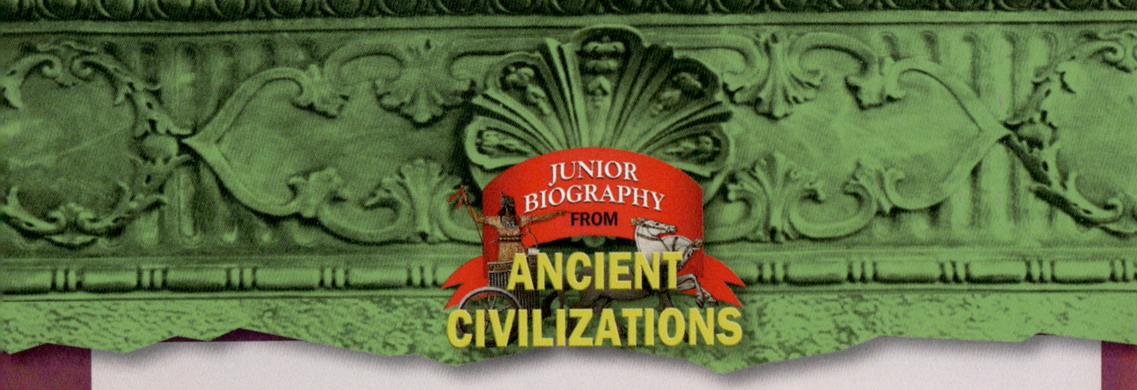

Alexander the Great • Archimedes • Augustus Caesar
Buddha • Charlemagne • Cleopatra • Confucius
Genghis Khan • Hammurabi • Hippocrates • Homer
Julius Caesar • King Arthur • Leif Erikson • Marco Polo
Moses • Nero • Plato • Pythagoras • Socrates

Copyright © 2018 by Mitchell Lane Publishers

All rights reserved. No part of this book may be reproduced without written permission from the publisher. Printed and bound in the United States of America.

ABOUT THE AUTHOR: Marcia Amidon Lusted has written over 100 books and 500 magazine articles for young readers. She lives in New Hampshire. Visit her at www.adventuresinnonfiction.com for more information about her books.

PUBLISHER'S NOTE: The facts on which the story in this book is based have been thoroughly researched. Documentation of such research can be found on pages 44–45. While every possible effort has been made to ensure accuracy, the publisher will not assume liability for damages caused by inaccuracies in the data, and makes no warranty on the accuracy of the information contained herein.

To reflect current usage, we have chosen to use the secular era designations BCE ("before the common era") and CE ("of the common era") instead of the traditional designations BC ("before Christ") and AD (*anno Domini,* "in the year of the Lord").

Printing 1 2 3 4 5 6 7 8 9

Library of Congress Cataloging-in-Publication Data

Names: Lusted, Marsha Amidon, author.
Title: Hippocrates / by Marsha Amidon Lusted.
Description: Hallandale, FL : Mitchell Lane Publishers, [2018] |
Series: Junior biography from ancient civilizations | Audience: Age 8-11. |
Audience: Grade 4 to 6. | Includes bibliographical references and index.
Identifiers: LCCN 2017009113 | ISBN 9781680200300 (library bound)
Subjects: LCSH: Hippocrates—Juvenile literature. | Medicine, Greek and Roman—Juvenile literature. | Physicians—Biography—Juvenile literature.
Classification: LCC R126.H8 L87 2018 | DDC 610.938 —dc23
LC record available at https://lccn.loc.gov/2017009113

eBook ISBN: 978-1-618020-031-7

CONTENTS

Phonetic pronunciations of words in **bold** can be found on page 46.

No one is exactly sure what Hippocrates looked like. This portrait is by Swiss painter Albert Andker (1831–1910).

CHAPTER 1
From Superstition to Science

Greece in much of the sixth and fifth centuries BCE was a place where great thinkers gathered and shared great ideas. This situation reached a peak in the city-state of Athens for several decades in the fifth century, which many historians refer to as the Golden Age of Greece. The most enduring symbol of this era was the Parthenon, a temple dedicated to the goddess Athena which still attracts visitors from all over the world. But for physicians who treated illnesses and injuries, it was also an era in which people believed in superstition, magic, and the whims of the gods when it came to their health.

Among those physicians was **Hippocrates***. Hippocrates did not believe that gods and their magic had anything to do with the health of the body and the onset of disease. "The gods simply cannot be held responsible for every ailment that afflicts human beings,"[1] he wrote. For example, some of his patients complained of stomach pains. Today this ailment is known as gastritis, and is treated with medicine or a change in diet. But most physicians of Hippocrates' time considered

*For pronunciations of words in **bold**, see page 46.

that stomach pain was the curse of the god **Apollo**. Why? Because one symptom of the disease was black bowel movements that looked like droppings of swallows. These birds were associated with Apollo, the god of medicine. Praying to Apollo provided the only method of obtaining relief.[2]

The Greeks also honored **Asclepius**, considered to be a master physician who could cure any ailment. Some stories even said that he had brought a dead man back to life. He supposedly inherited his medical knowledge from his father Apollo, but he himself was not a god because his mother was a mortal woman. When Asclepius died, Apollo grieved so much that he begged **Zeus**—the king of the gods—to honor Asclepius's memory. Zeus made Asclepius into the

This statue of the god Zeus is part of the Fountain of the Four Rivers in Rome, Italy.

Asclepius, the Greek god of medicine, is pictured here with Apollo and Hippocrates.

constellation **Ophiuchus** as well as making him the patron of all physicians.

Hippocrates knew that he could not change Greek society. But he wanted to show people that medicine was based on science, not superstition. He lived to the age of 80 or 90. During his long life, he would change the way that physicians thought about treating patients. He was the first Greek physician to look beyond magic and the gods and develop a system of medicine based on observation and common sense.[3]

Hippocrates and his beliefs guided physicians for thousands of years. Even today, new doctors take an oath based on Hippocrates' teachings and philosophy.

So what is known about this man and his life? How did he come to create such an important legacy?

HIPPOCRATES

Stone statue of Hippocrates by Alexander Munro at the Oxford University Museum of Natural History in Oxford, United Kingdom.

The Greek Gods

The Greeks believed in twelve gods who ruled over all aspects of human life. **Zeus** was the king of the gods. He was especially noted for hurling thunderbolts. **Hera** was the supreme goddess and the wife of Zeus. She was also the goddess of marriage and childbirth. **Poseidon** was the god of the sea. His weapon was a trident, which looked like a pitchfork with three prongs.

Hades was the lord of the underworld, and he ruled over the dead. He was also the god of wealth. **Hestia** was the goddess of the hearth and home. **Ares**, the son of Zeus and Hera, was the god of war.

Athena was the goddess of reason, intelligence, arts, and literature. **Apollo** was the god of music and healing. He taught medicine to mankind. His twin sister was **Artemis**, the goddess of hunting, the moon, and nature.

Aphrodite was the goddess of love, desire, and beauty. **Hermes** was the cleverest of the gods, and served as their messenger. Finally, **Hephaestus**, another son of Zeus and Hera, was the god of blacksmiths and craftspeople. Even though he was lame and deformed, he was Aphrodite's husband.

This marble image of the twelve gods and goddesses was probably created in the first century BCE. They all carry something that symbolizes their power.

Hippocrates' ideas were preserved through his writings and those of his students and followers.

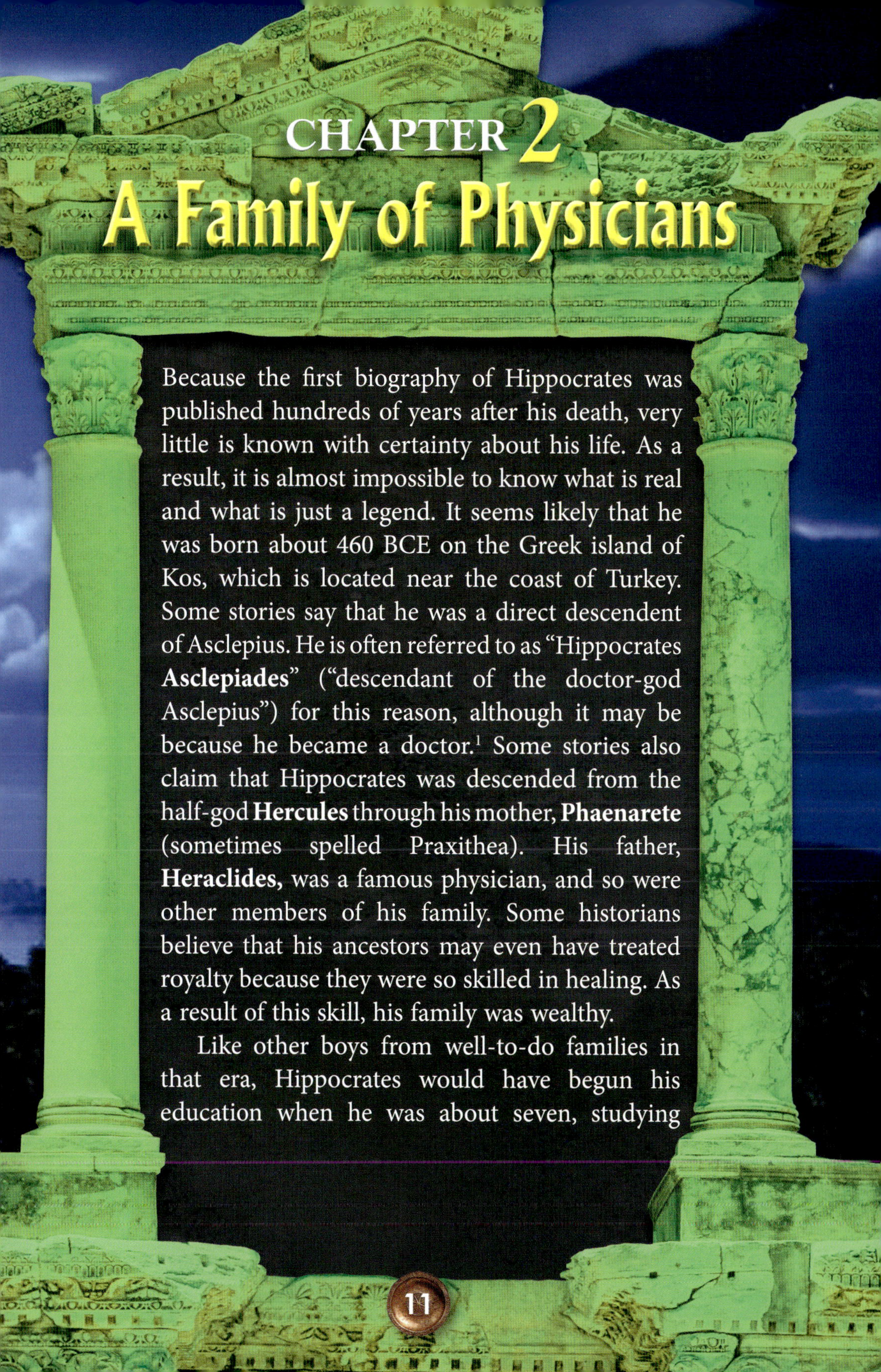

CHAPTER 2
A Family of Physicians

Because the first biography of Hippocrates was published hundreds of years after his death, very little is known with certainty about his life. As a result, it is almost impossible to know what is real and what is just a legend. It seems likely that he was born about 460 BCE on the Greek island of Kos, which is located near the coast of Turkey. Some stories say that he was a direct descendent of Asclepius. He is often referred to as "Hippocrates **Asclepiades**" ("descendant of the doctor-god Asclepius") for this reason, although it may be because he became a doctor.[1] Some stories also claim that Hippocrates was descended from the half-god **Hercules** through his mother, **Phaenarete** (sometimes spelled Praxithea). His father, **Heraclides,** was a famous physician, and so were other members of his family. Some historians believe that his ancestors may even have treated royalty because they were so skilled in healing. As a result of this skill, his family was wealthy.

Like other boys from well-to-do families in that era, Hippocrates would have begun his education when he was about seven, studying mathematics, religion, history, and music. Physical education was also an important part of school. Starting when he was about fifteen, Hippocrates would have spent several years in a secondary school, where there was even more focus on athletic training. Participating in sports also helped him understand more about how the human body worked, which would help him with his medical training.

From a very young age, Hippocrates learned about medicine from his father and grandfather. At first, he assisted his father in treating patients. He most likely did things like comforting patients suffering from extreme pain, running errands to get things like herbs and roots for treatments, and bringing equipment when his father needed it.

Some stories say that Hippocrates had a custom of going to the local market and watching the butchers at work slaughtering animals. He observed them as they skinned the carcasses and separated the fat and organs from the meat. In this way he could study the anatomy of these animals and the manner in which their bones, muscles, and organs were arranged. He also wondered about the anatomical similarities and differences between animals and humans.[2]

After he finished his secondary education, Hippocrates would have started working more closely with his father. He probably did this as an apprentice, a way of training for a career or skill through actual work experience. Hippocrates followed his father and another doctor, named **Herodicos**, who was from the Greek region of Thrace. He accompanied them as they went from patient to patient. He observed how they examined patients and diagnosed them, and then their treatments and what medicines they might prescribe. Hippocrates also traveled to the Greek mainland and possibly to places as far away as Egypt and Libya to practice medicine. He studied medicine in the Asclepium of Kos, a temple dedicated to Asclepius, on his home island.

From the time of his earliest training, Hippocrates was already thinking about medicine in a new way. He turned his back on the old superstitions about illness and the role of the gods. Instead, he was

Columns forming part of the Temple of Asclepius in Kos

thinking about medicine in terms of the human body and what it needed to function properly. Even as a teenager, he told his father, "If we could give every individual the right amount of nourishment and exercise, not too little and not too much, we would have found the safest way to health."[3] These ideas would form the foundation of his beliefs about medicine.

No one is exactly sure how old Hippocrates was when he began to practice medicine on his own. Apparently he quickly gained a reputation for the high quality of his work, and even outshone his father and Herodicos. Soon he would be practicing medicine all over Greece.

This bronze statue of Hippocrates shows him with two students and a woman seeking treatment for her child.

Ancient Greek Calendars

Dates in ancient Greece can be very confusing. Overall, the calendar might be similar from place to place, but each city-state had its own particular way of keeping track of days and dates. Like our modern calendar, the city-states shared a twelve-month system, though sometimes they added a thirteenth month when necessary.

However, the year itself started in different seasons depending on the location. In Athens, for example, the year began in early summer, while in Sparta, it began in the fall. The lengths of the months varied as well.

However, one method that historians use for dating events has to do with the Olympic Games, which began in 776 BCE and occurred every four years thereafter. Each four-year period from the end of one Olympics to the start of the next was called an Olympiad, and dates can be based on the Olympiad in which they took place. Using this dating system, historians believe that Hippocrates was born in the first year of the 80th Olympiad, or 460 BCE.

The city of Olympia in ancient Greece

In ancient Greece, dissecting a human body was forbidden and had to be carried out in secret.

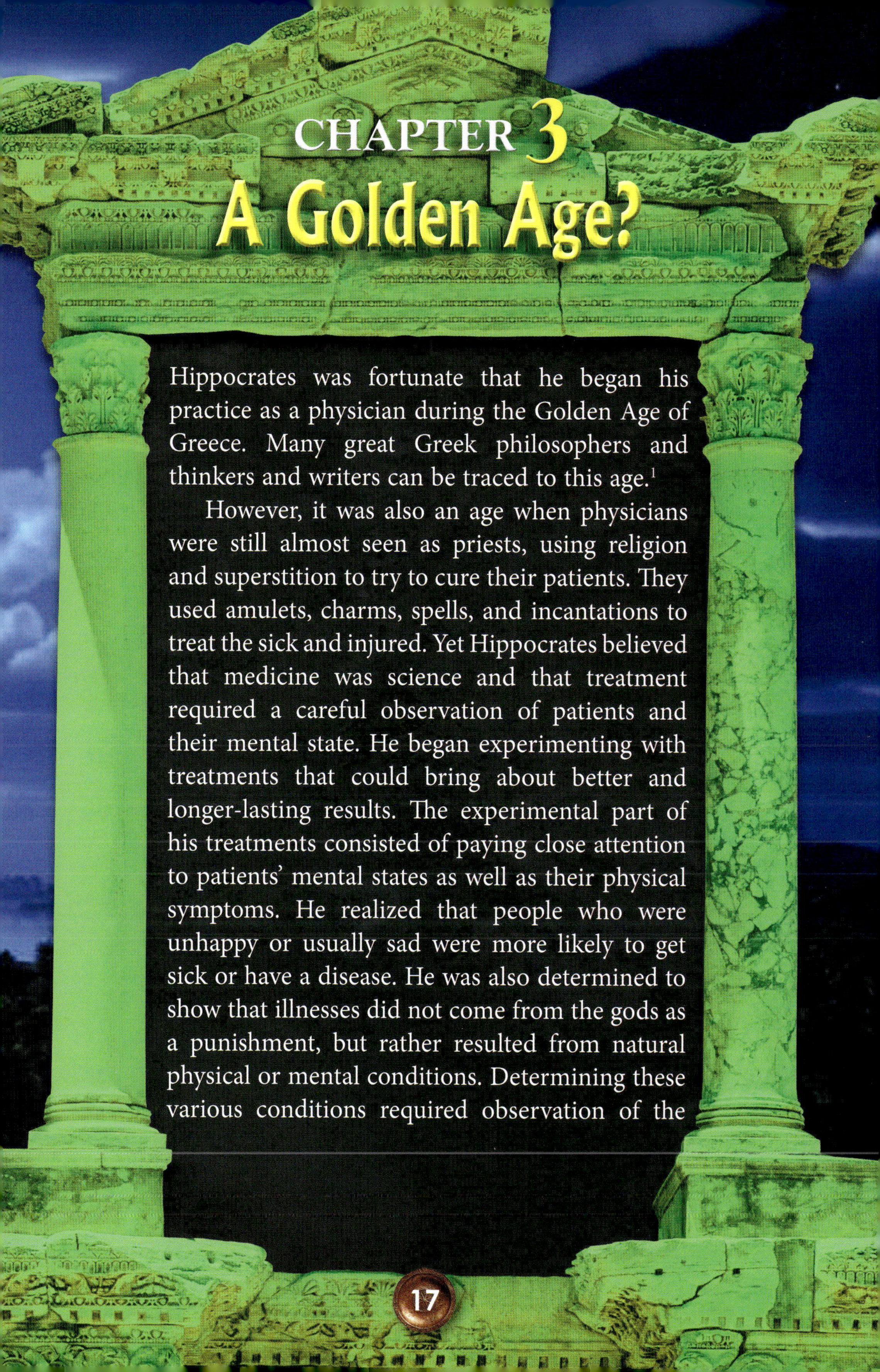

CHAPTER 3
A Golden Age?

Hippocrates was fortunate that he began his practice as a physician during the Golden Age of Greece. Many great Greek philosophers and thinkers and writers can be traced to this age.[1]

However, it was also an age when physicians were still almost seen as priests, using religion and superstition to try to cure their patients. They used amulets, charms, spells, and incantations to treat the sick and injured. Yet Hippocrates believed that medicine was science and that treatment required a careful observation of patients and their mental state. He began experimenting with treatments that could bring about better and longer-lasting results. The experimental part of his treatments consisted of paying close attention to patients' mental states as well as their physical symptoms. He realized that people who were unhappy or usually sad were more likely to get sick or have a disease. He was also determined to show that illnesses did not come from the gods as a punishment, but rather resulted from natural physical or mental conditions. Determining these various conditions required observation of the whole patient. Hippocrates wrote, "It is more important to know what sort of person has a disease than to know what sort of disease a person has."[2]

Hippocrates was limited by the knowledge of his time. The Greeks had immense respect for the human body, a respect that extended to death. They did not dissect corpses because that would have shown disrespect for the body. Hippocrates, therefore, had no way of knowing what the human body was like inside. He could only guess, based on his childhood observations of butchered animals. Anatomy and physiology were not well-developed sciences yet, so Hippocrates confused arteries, veins, and nerves and thought that muscles were the same as other kinds of flesh. But he did know that carefully observing patients—both the physical symptoms and their mental state—was very important in discovering the nature of their ailments and how best to treat them.

An example of Hippocrates' method of treatment involved a young man who came to him because of a large swelling in his lower back. Hippocrates examined the young man and concluded that the swelling was due to an infection resulting from significant amounts of pus in the lower lungs. He knew he would have to make an incision in the swelling to allow the pus to drain out. But where would he make the incision? Hippocrates applied a layer of wet clay to the infected area. He knew the infection would be worst in the place with the most heat, which would dry the clay fastest. He marked the spot where the clay dried first, cut into that spot, and drained the pus. He repeated this procedure for ten days, noting the color and odor of the discharge. Foul-smelling green pus meant there was still a life-threatening infection, while white pus without an aroma meant it was healing.[3]

However, basing medical treatment on natural causes and rather than religion or superstition made Hippocrates very controversial. His techniques conflicted with the procedures of the doctor-priests of the era. Many people viewed him as going against the will of the gods

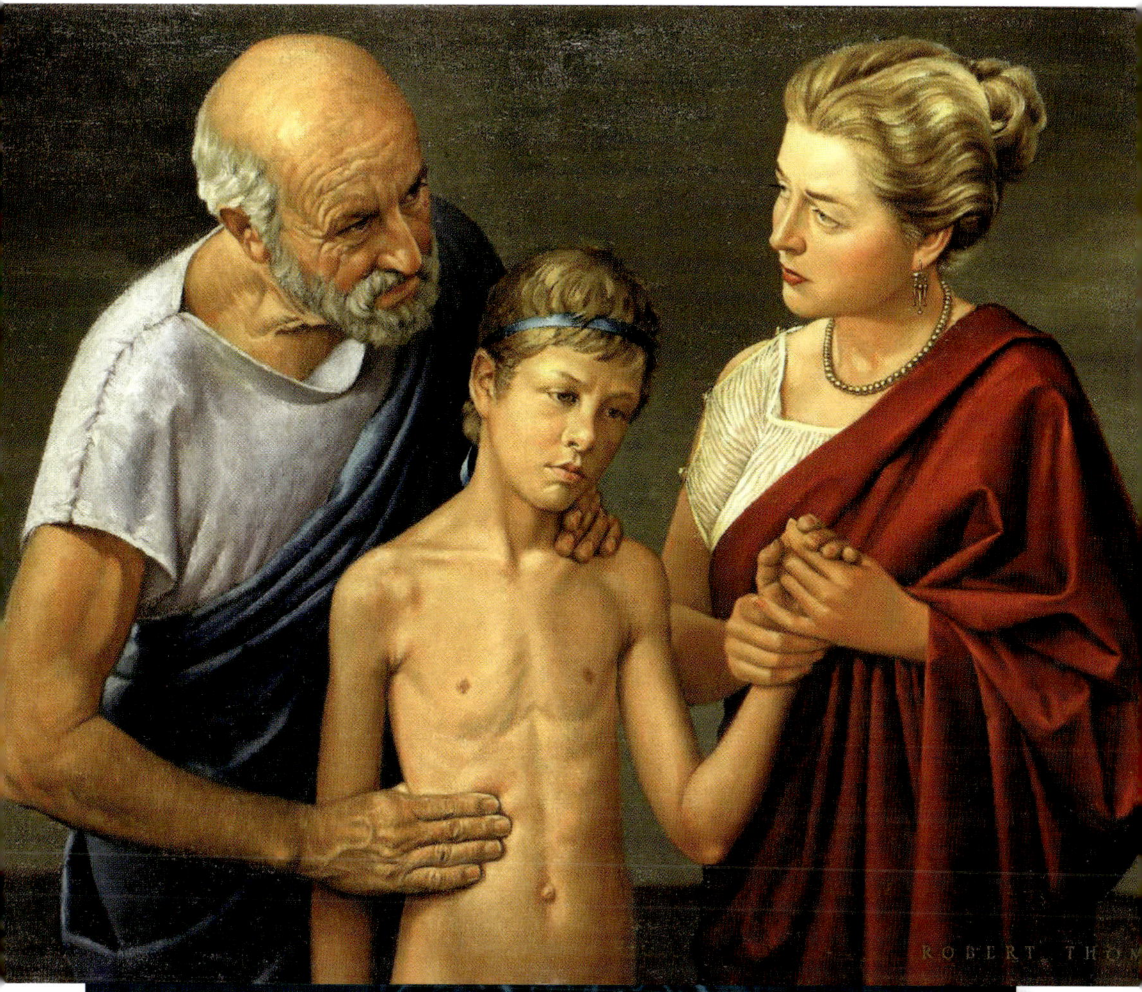

Hippocrates: Medicine Becomes a Science by American artist Robert Thom (1915–1979). Hippocrates examines a young patient, while reassuring his mother.

because he did not believe they were responsible for the afflictions of humans. Some sources maintain that he was sent to prison for a period of up to twenty years because of these conflicts. According to these sources, Hippocrates made the most of his time by treating his fellow prisoners. He observed their behavior, anatomy, symptoms, and when they had relapses of their diseases. He noted that prisoners suffered from mental problems and were more vulnerable to disease because they had been deprived of their freedom. He also realized that the filthy conditions in the prison played a role in spreading disease. He kept careful notes on all of his prison patients, building on his own medical knowledge and ideas.

It was during his time in prison that Hippocrates may have performed the first dissection of a human corpse. It would have given him valuable knowledge about how the human body works, but it was also a violation of the Greek taboo against dissection. As with so many aspects of Hippocrates' life, no one can be sure if this actually happened.

Hippocrates now had a wealth of medical knowledge and experience. Even though he may have been jailed, he was a respected physician. So how could he share his abilities and knowledge? Why is he still remembered today as the "Father of Modern Medicine?"

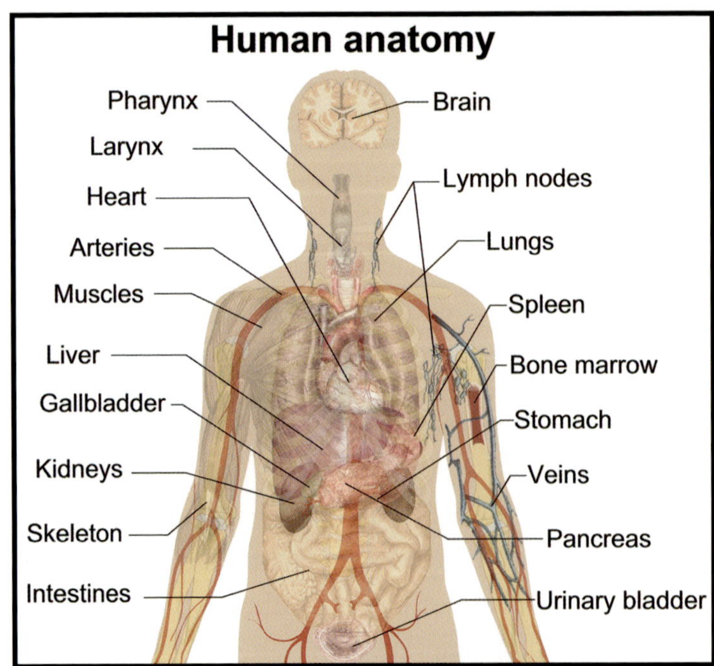

All humans have these basic body parts. Females and males also have separate organs that allow them to produce offspring.

Asclepia

Although Hippocrates was the first physician to base his diagnosis and treatments on observation rather than religion and superstition, he benefited from his training at the Asclepia of Kos. It was one of many asclepia that sprang up throughout Greece during and after Hippocrates' life.

These asclepia were basically hospitals that also included temples to Asclepius and relied on religious practices to promote healing. There were stories of people who awoke after a night in the asclepium to find that they had been miraculously cured. As these stories spread, more and more people went to the temples to be cured.

They maintained a system of casebooks, or records. These records were written on votive tablets (called pinake, or pinax if there was just one). A votive tablet was meant to be left in a temple as an offering, or in a tomb in memory of the person who had died. A pinax might even be written on a piece of cloth that could be hung on a wall.

A votive tablet of Asclepius

Patients left pinakes which included the symptoms, treatment, and results of their case as offerings to the god inside the temple. They would have provided Hippocrates with valuable information about illnesses and injuries and their treatments.

Hippocrates' legacy is honored all over the world, as seen by this statue in Brazil.

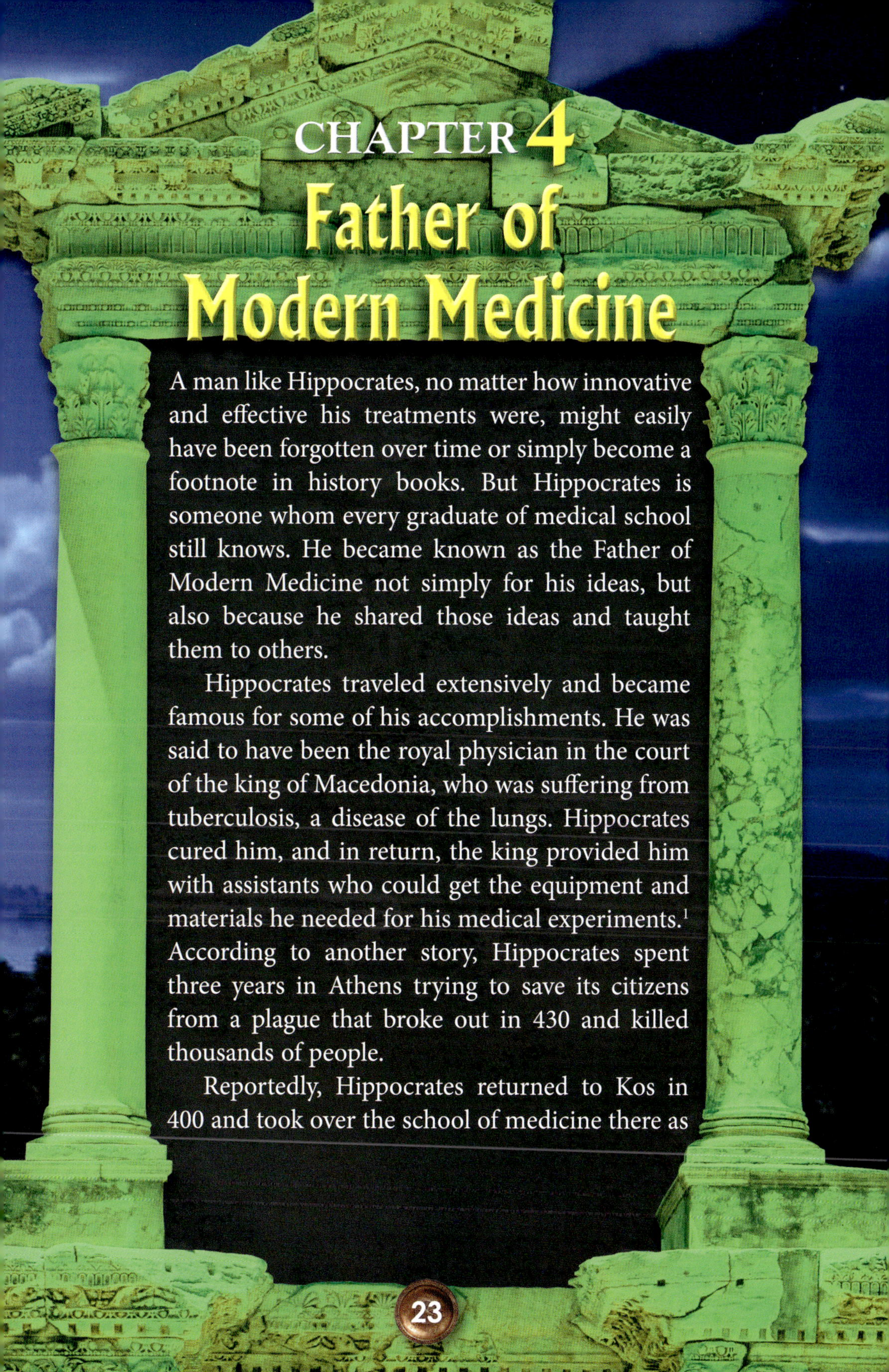

CHAPTER 4
Father of Modern Medicine

A man like Hippocrates, no matter how innovative and effective his treatments were, might easily have been forgotten over time or simply become a footnote in history books. But Hippocrates is someone whom every graduate of medical school still knows. He became known as the Father of Modern Medicine not simply for his ideas, but also because he shared those ideas and taught them to others.

Hippocrates traveled extensively and became famous for some of his accomplishments. He was said to have been the royal physician in the court of the king of Macedonia, who was suffering from tuberculosis, a disease of the lungs. Hippocrates cured him, and in return, the king provided him with assistants who could get the equipment and materials he needed for his medical experiments.[1] According to another story, Hippocrates spent three years in Athens trying to save its citizens from a plague that broke out in 430 and killed thousands of people.

Reportedly, Hippocrates returned to Kos in 400 and took over the school of medicine there as both a practicing doctor and a teacher. He apprenticed his own two sons, Thessalus and Draco, so they could learn about practicing medicine.

Soon Hippocrates was as famous for his teaching as he was for healing people. His school at Kos trained some of the most important medical scholars and doctors. They shared Hippocrates' teachings and ideas with others, as well as writing about what he taught.

Hippocrates was actually teaching a practice of medicine considerably different from the established way of thinking about medicine. Called the Cnidian school, it maintained that the human body was just a collection of isolated parts. When a person had a disease in a particular body part, the Cnidians would only treat that part. For example, patients with infected cuts on their feet would only be treated for that cut. If they also had a fever from the infection, a Cnidian doctor would see that as a completely different illness. They also relied on what the patient told them about how they were feeling, and did not include a close examination of the patient's symptoms.[2]

Hippocrates' school took a different approach. He saw the human body as a unified organism, and should be treated as a whole. A fever might be a symptom of an infection somewhere else in the body, and the fever couldn't be treated unless the infection itself was healed. Hippocrates did not just base his diagnosis and treatment on what the patient told him he was feeling. He carefully examined him for other signs of illness before deciding on a diagnosis. Hippocrates also believed that the main task for himself and other doctors was helping the natural processes of the body. The body wanted to fight against a disease, and the doctor was there to help it recover. Above all, the patient's environment was important to treating his disease. He wrote, "The physician must investigate the entire patient and his environment. Human health cannot be treated separately from the natural environment."[3] Because he believed that medicine should treat the whole patient and not just his or her disease, he also stressed the importance of a good diet, exercise, massage, and bathing in the ocean. He was reluctant to prescribe drugs or other medications and usually only gave the lowest possible dose. He created many techniques for performing surgery that were used for hundreds of years after his death.

Hippocrates helps a sick man during an epidemic of the plague.

One of his most enduring contributions was his role in creating the first system to explain the links between the human body, emotions, and health. According to this explanation, there were four humors in the body: black bile, yellow bile, phlegm, and blood. Each humor had specific qualities associated with it. Black bile was cold and dry, blood was hot and moist, phlegm was cold and moist, and yellow bile was hot and dry.

If these four humors were kept in balance, a person would be healthy. If they were out of balance, health problems would result. Too much black bile made a patient feel sad or depressed. Too much yellow bile might make a person restless and angry. It was the physician's job to bring the humors back into balance through diet, activity, and exercise.

One method of treatment tried to cure an excess of one humor by increasing the opposite humor. If a patient had a fever, which was a product of hot and dry yellow bile, the physician would prescribe cold baths to increase the opposite humor, which was cold and dry black bile.

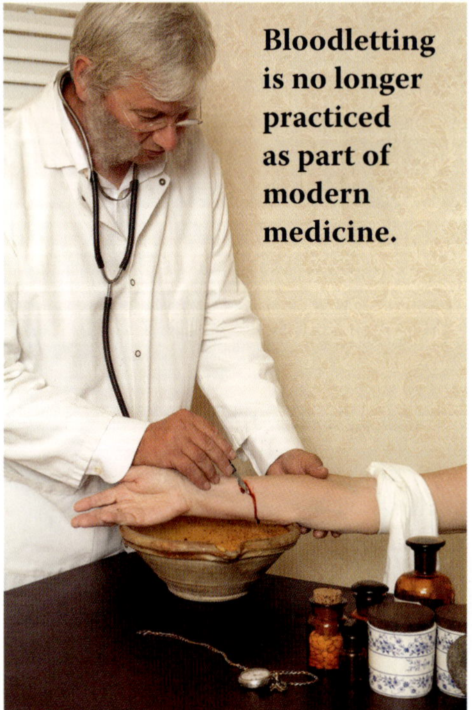

Bloodletting is no longer practiced as part of modern medicine.

Perhaps the most famous treatment method was bloodletting, which sought to cure an excess of blood by making an incision on the body and allowing a certain amount of blood to drain out. Or the physician might attach leeches to the patient. The creatures would drop off when they were full. Bloodletting remained a common medical practice well into the nineteenth century.

Hippocrates examines a patient with the help of his students and other physicians.

Asclepions such as this were temples to the god of medicine, Asclepius, as well as training facilities for students. Hippocrates is said to have received his medical training at an asclepion in Kos.

Hippocrates taught his students with a combination of clinical and physical examinations of patients, and explanations of his medical principles and theories. He observed illnesses closely and then created rules so the student physicians would know what to expect and what to do at the right time. His observations of diseases like malaria, tuberculosis, and pneumonia were written down in detailed case studies that would provide treatment guidelines for future doctors. He also felt sympathy for the sufferings of patients and stressed that the physician's place was at the bedside of his patient, observing and treating and trying to make them feel better.

Hippocrates not only taught his medical ideas and practices to the students of the medical school at Kos. His most famous legacy would be in writing.

Another view of Hippocrates' home island of Kos

The Hippocrates Tree

One of the most famous symbols of Hippocrates' role as a teacher is the Hippocrates Tree on Kos. Stories say that Hippocrates used to gather his students beneath an oriental plane tree in the center of the island.

There is still a Hippocrates Plane Tree on Kos today, although this tree is only about 500 years old. It is said to be a descendent of the original tree, and is protected by a metal fence.

This tree has relatives all over the world. Its cuttings and seeds have been given as gifts to medical schools in places like the United States, England, Scotland, and Australia.

One tree, planted at the National Library of Medicine near Washington, DC, in 1962, has actually had its DNA preserved and recorded for the future. Scientists there feel that Hippocrates himself would have been fascinated by the idea of DNA and how it can help in understanding and treating human disease.

The Hippocrates Tree in the town of Kos

Images of Hippocrates often appear on medical buildings, such as the Stuyvesant Polyclinic Hospital in New York City shown here.

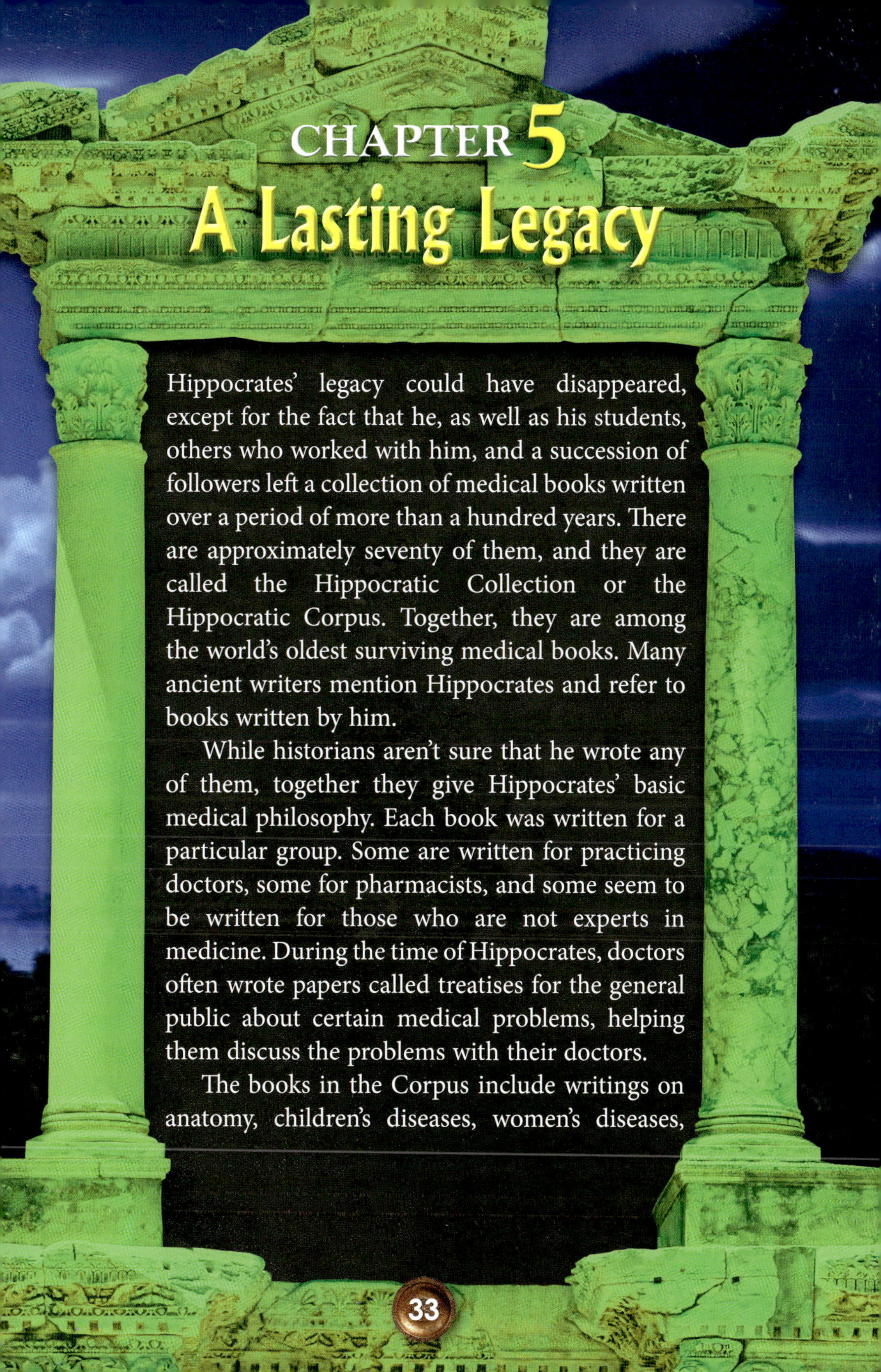

CHAPTER 5
A Lasting Legacy

Hippocrates' legacy could have disappeared, except for the fact that he, as well as his students, others who worked with him, and a succession of followers left a collection of medical books written over a period of more than a hundred years. There are approximately seventy of them, and they are called the Hippocratic Collection or the Hippocratic Corpus. Together, they are among the world's oldest surviving medical books. Many ancient writers mention Hippocrates and refer to books written by him.

While historians aren't sure that he wrote any of them, together they give Hippocrates' basic medical philosophy. Each book was written for a particular group. Some are written for practicing doctors, some for pharmacists, and some seem to be written for those who are not experts in medicine. During the time of Hippocrates, doctors often wrote papers called treatises for the general public about certain medical problems, helping them discuss the problems with their doctors.

The books in the Corpus include writings on anatomy, children's diseases, women's diseases, how to predict the progress of a disease or illness, treatments of conditions based on diet and medication, surgery, and medical ethics. Also included were works on meteorology, climate, anthropology, and geography as they related to medicine and health. There is a book called *Aphorisms*, a collection of wise sayings about diet and medicine. These sayings included "Too much sleep and too much wakefulness are both bad" and "Science produces knowledge, opinion [produces] ignorance."[1] Another one is *Ancient Medicine*, which compared Hippocrates' approach to medicine with ancient approaches.

It is because of the Hippocratic Corpus that Hippocrates' ideas have lasted so long. He died about 370 in Larissa, Greece (though as with other aspects of life no one knows exactly the year of his death). His methods and principles had gained popularity as he grew older, and after his death his students and followers were determined to preserve his legacy by collecting and writing down his knowledge. In fact, Hippocrates' teachings were so widely accepted that medical knowledge actually stalled after his death, since it was felt that his ideas were too great to be improved on. It wasn't until the Greek physician Galen practiced and wrote about Hippocratic medicine in the latter part of second century CE that more progress was made. In medieval and Renaissance Europe, Hippocratic techniques were once again used and improved on.

Hippocrates' legacy carries down even to the present day. New doctors who graduate from medical school usually take what is called the Hippocratic Oath. The modern version says, in part:

> I will respect the hard-won scientific gains of those physicians in whose steps I walk, and gladly share such knowledge as is mine with those who are to follow.
>
> I will apply, for the benefit of the sick, all measures [that] are required, avoiding those twin traps of overtreatment and therapeutic nihilism.

A fragment of the Hippocratic Oath, written on papyrus

This mural, painted in Italy in the 12th century, shows the physician Galen (left) talking with Hippocrates.

EX hIS FOR
MANTRQVE
VNT QVE
TVR

I will remember that there is art to medicine as well as science, and that warmth, sympathy, and understanding may outweigh the surgeon's knife or the chemist's drug.

I will not be ashamed to say "I know not," nor will I fail to call in my colleagues when the skills of another are needed for a patient's recovery.[2]

Hippocrates is not only called The Father of Modern Medicine because he changed the way that the world viewed disease and treatment. He was also the ideal physician: wise, caring, and honest. His oath sets the same high standards for all modern doctors, and his life has inspired doctors and healers for over two thousand years.

This funeral monument of Hippocrates is located on the road leading to Larissa, where he died.

The Old Oath

The Hippocratic Oath that new doctors take today is not the same as the classical version that dates back to ancient times. That version contains a number of differences. Here are a few.

> I swear by Apollo Physician and Asclepius and **Hygieia** and **Panaceia** and all the gods and goddesses, making them my witnesses, that I will fulfill according to my ability and judgment this oath and this covenant:
>
> I will neither give a deadly drug to anybody who asked for it, nor will I make a suggestion to this effect. In purity and holiness I will guard my life and my art.
>
> If I fulfill this oath and do not violate it, may it be granted to me to enjoy life and art, being honored with fame among all men for all time to come; if I transgress it and swear falsely, may the opposite of all this be my lot.[3]

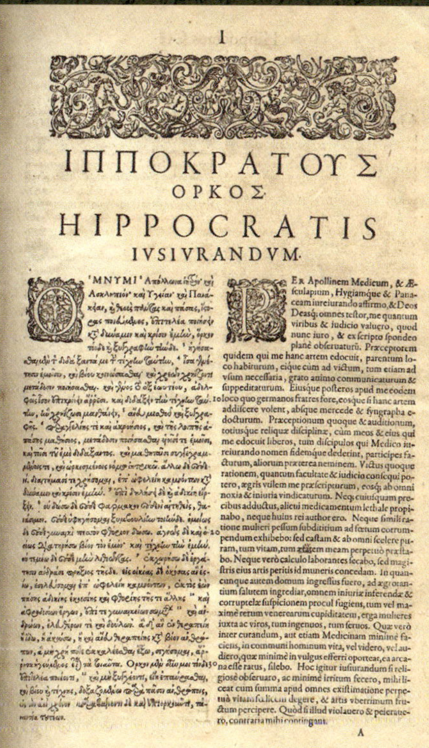

I

ΙΠΠΟΚΡΑΤΟΥΣ
ΟΡΚΟΣ

HIPPOCRATIS
IVSIVRANDVM.

PEr Apollinem Medicum, & Æsculapium, Hygiamque & Panaceam iureiurando affirmo, & Deos Deasq; omnes testor, me quantum viribus & iudicio valuero, quod nunc iuro, & ex scripto spondeo planè obseruaturũ. Præceptorem quidem qui me hanc artem edocuit, parentum loco habiturum, eique cùm ad victum, tum etiam ad vsum necessaria, grato animo communicaturum & suppeditaturum. Eiusque posteros apud me eodem loco quo germanos fratres fore, eosque si hanc artem addiscere volent, absque mercede & syngrapha edocturum. Præceptionum quoque & auditionum, totiusque reliquæ disciplinæ, cùm meos & eius qui me edocuit liberos, tum discipulos qui Medico iureiurando nomen fidemque dederint, participes facturum, aliorum prætereà neminem. Victus quoque rationem, quantum facultate & iudicio consequi potero, ægris vtilem me præscripturum, eosq; ab omni noxia & iniuria vindicaturum. Neq; cuiusquam precibus adductus, alicui medicamentum lethale propinabo, neque huius rei author ero. Neque simili ratione mulieri pessum subdititium ad fœtum corrumpendum exhibebo: sed castam & ab omni scelere puram, tum vitam, tum artem meam perpetuò præstabo. Neque verò calculo laborantes secabo, sed magistris eius artis peritis id muneris concedam. In quancunque autem domum ingressus fuero, ad ægrotantium salutem ingrediar, omnem iniuriæ inferendæ & corruptelæ suspicionem procul fugiens, tum vel maximè rerum venerearum cupiditatem, erga mulieres iuxta ac viros, tum ingenuos, tum seruos. Quæ verò inter curandum, aut etiam Medicinam minimè faciens, in communi hominum vita, vel videro, vel audiero, quæ minimè in vulgus efferri oporteat, ea arcana esse ratus, silebo. Hoc igitur iusiurandum si religiosè obseruaro, ac minimè irritum fecero, mihi liceat cum summa apud omnes existimatione perpetuò vitam fœliciter degere, & artis vberrimum fructum percipere. Quòd si illud violauero & peierauero, contraria mihi contingant.

A

This text of the Hippocratic Oath is written in both Greek and Latin.

The old version of the oath is written in more formal language. It also refers to the gods and goddesses. Today's doctors come from many different religions, so the oath doesn't refer to deities anymore. Doctors also practice medicine for reasons other than honor and fame. The new oath, therefore, reflects modern times and modern life.

This map shows many of the important places in Hippocrates' life.

Because so little is known about Hippocrates' life, all dates are approximate.

BCE	
460	Hippocrates is born on the island of Kos, in Greece.
445	Hippocrates attends secondary school.
443	Hippocrates apprentices under his father, and travels to the Greek mainland, Egypt, and Libya.
430	Hippocrates begins combating the plague in Athens.
400	Hippocrates takes over the medical school at Kos.
370	Hippocrates dies at Larissa, Greece.

TIMELINE

BCE	
ca. 600	The rise of Greek science and philosophy begins.
508	Kleisthenes reforms the Athenian code of laws, and establishes a democratic constitution.
495	Athenian statesman Pericles, the leader during the Golden Age, is born.
490	An outnumbered Athenian army defeats invading Persians at the Battle of Marathon.
479	Greek victory at the Battle of Plataea ends the Persian threat and ushers in the Golden Age.
447	Athenians begin construction of the Parthenon, the famous temple of Athena.
431	The Peloponnesian War pits Athens and its allies against Sparta and its allies; it lasts for 27 years.
430	A plague breaks out in Athens and kills thousands of people.
334	Alexander the Great begins ten-year military campaign that includes Egypt, India, and the Middle East and spreads Greek culture and learning.
331	Alexander founds the city of Alexandria in Egypt; it becomes the center for Greek scholarship and medicine.
323	Alexander dies.
146	Roman forces invade Greece

CE	
ca. 160	The Greek physician Galen begins carrying on Hippocrates' work.
ca. 900	Arab scholars become very interested in Hippocrates and the Hippocratic Collection.
ca. 1900	Bloodletting as a method of treating disease comes to an end.

Chapter 1: From Superstition to Science

1. Rosalie F. Baker and Charles F. Baker III, *Ancient Greeks: Creating the Classical Tradition* (New York, NY: Oxford University Press, 1997), p. 116.
2. Ibid.
3. "Hippocrates," NNDB. www.nndb.com/people/680/000087419/

Chapter 2: A Family of Physicians

1. "Hippocrates Biography," Encyclopedia of World Biography. www.notablebiographies.com/He-Ho/Hippocrates.html
2. "Hippocrates," Simply Knowledge. http://www.simplyknowledge.com/biographies/hippocrates
3. Ibid.

Chapter 3: The Golden Age

1. Rosalie F. Baker and Charles F. Baker III, *Ancient Greeks: Creating the Classical Tradition* (New York, NY: Oxford University Press, 1997), p. 97.
2. "Hippocrates," Simply Knowledge. http://www.simplyknowledge.com/biographies/hippocrates
3. Baker, *Ancient Greeks*, pp. 117–118.

Chapter 4: Father of Modern Medicine

1. Hippocrates," Simply Knowledge. http://www.simplyknowledge.com/biographies/hippocrates
2. David K. Osborn, "Who's Who in Greek Medicine: Hippocrates." Greek Medicine.net. www.greekmedicine.net/whos_who/Hippocrates.html
3. Spyros G. Marketos, "History of Medicine." http://asclepieion.mpl.uoa.gr/parko/marketos2.htm

Chapter 5: A Lasting Legacy

1. Rosalie F. Baker and Charles F. Baker III, *Ancient Greeks: Creating the Classical Tradition* (New York, NY: Oxford University Press, 1997), pp. 116–117.
2. Peter Tyson, "The Hippocratic Oath Today." PBS Nova, March 27, 2001. http://www.pbs.org/wgbh/nova/body/hippocratic-oath-today.html
3. Ibid.

Books

Bordessa, Kris. *Tools of the Ancient Greeks: A Kid's Guide to the History & Science of Life in Ancient Greece*. White River Junction, VT: Nomad Press, 2006.

Gow, Mary. *The Greatest Doctor of Ancient Times: Hippocrates and His Oath*. Berkeley Heights, NJ: Enslow Publishers, 2009.

Jankowski, Connie. *Hippocrates: Father of Medicine*. Minneapolis, MN: Capstone, 2009.

Pearson, Anne. *Eyewitness Books Ancient Greece*. New York: DK Publishing, 2007.

Whiting, Jim. *Hippocrates*. Hockessin, DE: Mitchell Lane Publishing, 2006.

On the Internet

Kidipede: Ancient Greek Medicine
http://www.historyforkids.org/learn/greeks/science/medicine/

Hippocrates
http://greekphysician.weebly.com/biography.html

Kids Work!: History of Medicine
http://www.knowitall.org/kidswork/hospital/history/ancient/

National Institutes of Health: Greek Medicine
http://www.nlm.nih.gov/hmd/greek/greek_rationality.html

Works Consulted

"The Ancient Greek Calendar." Polysyllabic.com.
http://www.polysyllabic.com/?q=calhistory/earlier/greek

Baker, Rosalie F. and Charles F. Baker III, *Ancient Greeks: Creating the Classical Tradition*. New York, NY: Oxford University Press, 1997.

"Biography: Hippocrates." Greek Physician.com.
http://greekphysician.weebly.com/biography.html

Dublin, Marc. "Introduction: Kos—Island of Hippocrates." Matt Barrett's Travel Guides: Greek Travel. http://www.greektravel.com/greekislands/kos/

"Hippocrates Biography." Encyclopedia of World Biography. http://www.notablebiographies.com/He-Ho/Hippocrates.html

"Hippocrates Plane Tree." Greeka.com. http://www.greeka.com/dodecanese/kos/kos-excursions/kos-hippocrates-plane-tree.htm

"Hippocrates." NNDB. http://www.nndb.com/people/680/000087419/

"Hippocrates." Simply Knowledge. http://simplyknowledge.com/biographies/hippocrates

"Hippocrates." The Famous People. http://www.thefamouspeople.com/profiles/hippocrates-120.php

Marketos, Spyros G. "History of Medicine: The Medical School of Cos, Hippocratic Medicine." University of Athens Medical School. http://asclepieion.mpl.uoa.gr/parko/marketos2.htm

O'Brien, Jane. "DNA fingerprint for Hippocrates' legendary tree." BBC News, April 28, 2014. http://www.bbc.com/news/science-environment-27190148

Osborn, David K. "Hippocrates: Father of Medicine." Greek Medicine.net. http://www.greekmedicine.net/whos_who/Hippocrates.html

PHONETIC PRONUNCIATIONS

Aphrodite (af-roh-DIE-tee)

Asclepia (as-KLEE-pee-uh)

Asclepiades (as-KLEE-pee-a-deez)

Asclepius (as-KLEE-pee-uhs)

Athena (a-THEE-na)

Apollo (a-POL-lo)

Ares (AIR-eez)

Artemis (AHR-tuh-mis)

Hades (HAY-deez)

Hephaestus (huh-FES-tuhs)

Hera (HIR-uh)

Heraclides (hir-ACK-lu-deez)

Hercules (HUR-kyoo-leez)

Hestia (HES-tee-uh)

Hermes (HER-meez)

Herodicos (her-OH-dik-os)

Hippocrates (hih-poh-KRAH-teez)

Hygieia (hy-JEE-uh)

Ophiuchus (of-ee-YOO-kuhs)

Panaceia (pan-uh-SEE-ya)

Phaenarete (fen-uhr-REE-tee)

Poseidon (puh-SY-duhn)

Zeus (ZOO-s)

PHOTO CREDITS: Cover, p. 1, 14—cc-by sa 3.0; p. 4—Albert Anker/public domain; p. 6—Thinkstock/Joan Coll; pp. 7, 35—Wellcome Library, London/cc-by sa 4.0; p. 8—Oxford University Museum of Natural History/cc-by sa 3.0; p. 9—Walters Art Museum/public domain; p. 10—Stock Montage/Getty Images; p. 13—Thinkstock/modustollens; p. 15—public domain; pp. 16, 39—U.S. National Library of Medicine/National Institute of Health.gov; p. 19—Robert Thom/UMHS; p. 20—Mikael Häggström/public domain; p. 21—European Virtual Museum; p. 22—Thiago Vieira/cc-by 2.0; p. 25—akg-images/Newscom; p. 26—Photowitch/Dreamstime; p. 27—Album/Prisma/Newscom; pp. 28–29—Thinkstock/PanosKarapanagiotis; p. 30—Thinkstock/tella_db; p. 31—Actiacti/Dreamstime; p. 33—Tony Fischer/cc-by 2.0; pp. 36–37—Holly Hayes/cc-by 2.0; p. 38—Thinkstock/Yoeml; p. 40—Andrea Pickens.

GLOSSARY

ailment (ALE-ment)—a body disorder or sickness
anatomy (uh-NAT-uh-mee)—the structural makeup of an organism or any of its parts
carcass (CAR-cuss)—a dead body; especially the body of a meat animal prepared for market
city-state (SIH-tee STATE)—a self-governing area consisting of a city and the surrounding territory
contagious (con-TAY-juss)—able to be passed on by contact between individuals
controversial (con-truh-VER-see-uhl)—something about which there is great difference of opinion that causes a long or heated discussion
democracy (deh-MAH-cruh-see)—government in which the supreme power is held by the people and used by them directly or indirectly through representation
diagnose (die-ig-NOZE)—to recognize a disease or disorder by signs and symptoms
dialect (DIE-uh-lekt)—a variety of a language used by the members of a particular group or class
dissection (dis-SEK-shun)—the act of cutting up a plant, animal, or human body into separate parts for examination and study
DNA—any of various nucleic acids resembling a flexible twisted ladder located in cell nuclei that determine a person's heredity.
ethics (ETH-iks)—the rules of moral conduct governing an individual or a group
incision (in-SIH-zuhn)—a cut made into the body during surgery
legacy (LEG-uh-see)—something left to a person or a group
organism (OR-gun-izm)—something having many related parts that function together as a whole
patron (PAY-trun)—a person who gives generous support or approval
pharmacist (FAHR-muh-sist)—someone trained in the practice of preparing drugs according to a doctor's prescription
philosophy (fil-OSS-uh-fee)—the study of basic ideas about knowledge, truth, right and wrong, religion, and the nature and meaning of life
physiology (fih-zee-AH-luh-gee)—the life processes and activities of a living thing or any of its parts
superstition (soo-per-STISH-uhn)—a belief or practice resulting from ignorance, fear of the unknown, or trust in magic
treatise (TREE-tuss)—a book or article examining a subject carefully and completely